PRAISE FOR UNEX

Shortlisted for the 2021 National Trans

Shortlisted for the The Sarah Maguire Prize for Poetry in Translation 2022

'With lines like "Shall we fill our mouths with cherries and kiss naughtily knottily all night long", Lee Hyemi's poetry, bewitchingly translated by Soje, makes me shiver with pleasure. To taste *Unexpected Vanilla* is to take a midnight dip in a deep, dark pool. Thrilling, sexy and subversive, it refuses to give up its secrets easily. I'm obsessed.' – Shu-Ling Chua, author of *Echoes*

'*Unexpected Vanilla* is a collection filled with female sensuality and wondrous longings. I adore Lee's adventurous exploration of the mundane – how a weather can be personal, a bunch of grapes in a bowl of water can be an underwater jungle. This collection is diary-like, scattered with understated eroticism. It is also playful and experimental. In Lee's poetry, there is little distinction between bodies and nature. We are all but fluid breaths – "the knots of air,/jumbled and suspended,/deepen and seep into each other." The barriers between language and Language melt away in this masterfully translated work of poetry.' – Jinhao Xie, as seen in Poetry Foundation, *Bitter Melon Press* and *bath magg*

'In Lee Hyemi's work, the body is a liquid, mutable, flickering thing. These vulnerable poems shimmer and surge with a yearning for the natural world, transcendence and communion. A fresh and refreshing voice.' – Remi Graves, author of *with your chest*

'A sensuous poetry collection full of mouths licking, parting, kissing, whispering, Lee Hyemi's *Unexpected Vanilla* shows how delicious the language of desire and intimacy can be. Soje's fantastic translation astutely brings out the wordplay and queer sexuality embedded in the source text.' – Emily Jungmin Yoon, author of *A Cruelty Special to Our Species and Ordinary Misfortunes*

'"This is the story of two equal tongue-tips, / of white double flowers laid on lips," says Lee Hyemi, in an exquisite rendition of her voice into English by her translator Soje. Sensual beauty is suffused throughout *Unexpected Vanilla*, and its record of desires melt boundaries of flesh and soul. Here, the poet and her translator match their tongue-tips, and flowers emerge from their lips.' – Jack Jung, co-translator of *Yi Sang: Selected Works*

'In this book, a comma, a line break or a period are like cat doors that lead us to worlds of the strange. Brilliant, remarkable and fun in its play on images and structures, this book is truly unputdownable.' – Norman Erikson Pasaribu, author of *Happy Stories, Mostly*

'I think of Lee Hyemi's *Unexpected Vanilla*, in translation by Soje, as a kind of hydration after the extended hangover of this year. The poems, which have been called surrealist and sensual, are what I've been turning to when feeling life-parched by the constant interventions in intimacy produced by screens and masks, as well as those greater interventions produced and reproduced by gender binaries and heteropatriarchy.' – Kaitlin Rees, *AJAR Press*

'Lee's poetry is a revelry in writing in and of a state of pre-position and "until-ness."' – Liam Bishop, *Hong Kong Review of Books*

UNEXPECTED

VANILLA

TRANSLATED BY

UNEXPECTED VANILLA

LEE HYEMI

SOJE

TILTED AXIS PRESS

There is always an exchange of fluids
at the critical moment when a relationship deepens.
Holding the fish jar in which alphabets swim
I step into the world of the second person.

SUMMER, WHEN LOQUATS LIGHT UP

Let's walk with our fingers laced when the loquats arrive. Wet trees permeating between each finger. When we become jumbled branches with all the yellow we have, our touching palms become the world's ripped interior. A tree begins when you break the berry and wet some other flesh. That's why people who've put their palm lines together travel inside the same dream.

As our arms start to fall back to our sides, we rub our fibrous skin and smell summer spreading through the air. The vibrations rising brilliantly between each tree. Open the jiggling fleshy fruits and listen to the sound of countless white bells clanging against each other. While the leaves nip the open air with their new front teeth.

We become newly sprouted violins and clear our surroundings. A tree's determination to empty the space between each branch, like parted fingers touching the world at last. When we produce a single superimposed seed with all the bones we have, we hear the season we entrusted arriving inside the luminous yellow.

ARRIVING LIGHTS

Lights were born as I opened my eyes

Someone fogged up my window after leaving their shadow
behind last night I unraveled dream-bouquets that died
down in a whirlwind The lights headed towards humans
must still be lost in a distant light-year because

the twinkle in my eyes tremble with the intuition of an incoming
planet When flocks of light flying high on eyelashes find a
place to settle, a landscape is born

Like an impulse surging in the dark,

I flipped the shaded room into a bright sphere and found a world
reachable by trace alone Just as sleep collects in the corners
of closed eyes or distant light travels to sway in front of taut
lashlines,

some lights shine more vividly when they're gone When I
washed the dewy planet and set it on a sunny windowsill, a
human silhouette swayed above my closed eyes

WORLD OF BREATHS

Whoever has ever put their hand under the nose
of a sleeping person believes in souls Deep at night
breaths drift past a forest and flow in the mud,
returning soaked and weary

If you weave the rays of respiration,
joining your breaths with the sleeper's
as if retracing footprints that have started to melt,

inside is the blazing forest
outside is the whirling blizzard

Like birds, breaths fly
in between the two
like planets suddenly entering another orbit

Some things you only hear at dawn, asleep embraced:
the sound of a dry leaf gently
falling on a white field,
the sound of a single wheel
stroking a wet ear

Watching the abyss constantly be reborn
lightly, weakly, clearly

you erase your face
The knots of air,
jumbled and suspended,
deepen and seep into each other

DIVER

We've talked about the hand that pushes the head down. The massive body of water, the gaze of the deep silent sea. The faraway ocean floor that resolutely spouts darkness wherever it casts its gaze.

The ocean was neither its floor nor the three dimensions of water, but merely the earth's ceiling. Like a hand extended to change a light bulb we lined our bodies abreast and went to find the light said to be the darkest.

I open my mouth wide and kiss the still-remaining atmosphere. Humans forget how to speak with only a kiss. Abandon your words and dive into the mouth's deep ocean ... That's either the ceiling of a person or the floor of an afternoon. The lining of the luminous overcoat worn by the Earth.

About the space where the air bubbles inside the body rapidly expand, where interior and exterior invade each other. About the allied forces of color and pressure that a human body must endure.

We've talked about them before. We rise to an unfamiliar surface. That was us turning over the ocean cultivated long inside our bodies and offering it to each other.

BANAN

Banan, with the touch of two clasped hands

mangled incantations parted the lips to spill out When soft stems
sprout from an abandoned grave, when buried hands are soil-
stained up to the wrists, blotted fingers dig into the body's
deepest corners Because the hands' direction determines the
prayer's whereabouts and an earnest plea is the secret crack
in the door that redeems the hands' darkness

Where have the foreign fruits spilling unfamiliar scents gone? Or
the prayer that created a new species by burying the lover's
severed hands?

Banan, listen to the heart leaking through the clenched hands
and pluck the rotting fingers one by one A small soft bone
must be sprouting even from the flowerpot where a person
is planted The sensation of this gentle handshake rises into
the missing fruit-flesh

CENOTE

The ceiling sank when the mouth opened. Streams surged, and a
luminous tunnel appeared on the ground. Where did it go?
Murky dim things strewed the water's surface.

After sweeping the moon with my hand, I peered into a dizzying
flower and found its fearful crowded core. Lights narrowing
toward that single dot. White arrows being shot at the
undulating ground.

Can I call them wings? Letters I scribbled while falling, papers
peeking from ripped envelopes. Sucked into a bottomless
song, time turned its back into the darkest farewell. Can I
call it a hole that reflects darkness? Or a well that draws up
the moon?

Lying inside a mill and waiting for another light, I felt a stream
of water passing through my body. It was the river coursing
toward the moon, the inside of a grave turned out and bright.

POLAR NIGHT

The bell-ringer departed by night A distant bonfire was reflected
in the window that glimmered whenever I locked all the
doors and talked to myself Only then did winter begin A
deep winter I wouldn't have known otherwise

Did you burn sweet olive branches and stroke fragrant grass,
then dig through the fire-dyed wood with those same hands?
The air is thick with smoke and scent from across the river
Who is it? Who dyes my eyebrows with dregs of snow, even
from that unreachable place?

Lighting a match with frozen fingers, I think of the red liquor
promising Christmas There were sounds we heard in the
distance that opened the window every hour and called to
fleeing birds, that smelled the breath of blazing trees held in
nonexistent arms

There was a bonfire beyond this place Too distant to go and find,
too cold to idly watch from afar

Shattered snowflakes crunch inside my mouth Tossing black
bones out the window I mutter Dear wanderer who
stumbled out of view with a broken bell in your arms for the
things I wouldn't have known in the dark, things that linger
then set like the sun You who carried sound this far, then
entered two small pocket-like ears

My love who cannot hear, as you burned your eyes and lips on
the fading light, there was neither bell-ringer nor a bell to
break yet a lone toll tore through the frozen sheet of sky

THE CUPBOARD WITH STRAWBERRY JAM

We stood on our tiptoes and fumbled around the top shelf for a taste of those red red things. With mouths dyed all over, feeling like a pair of nipples.

Unni, we must be one person, cunningly divergent. The morning we wore the disheveled green crowns of strawberries and spoke of our first wet dreams under the covers. We laid a chewy seed in every pore, growing recklessly private and gradually tender. In the kingdom for two who sway inside translucent jelly.

If I had a spare season, I would've rushed to whisper vulgar words like a bird with a disappearing beak and gifted you the sweetest song on the verge of rot. I would've squished the all-pink rainbow and called the morning owl over with the strange joy of guilt.

Feeling like there was more to hide now as the sweet stickiness dripped between our fingers. If we had another pair of lips, another pair of thin mucous membranes, we could've talked about the flavors that deepen as they're mixed.

But today, simply with our arms spread wide, we experienced our ruddiness of old. Of the days when we loved what was hidden and sweet.

A POPPY'S SUMMER

Dripping white resin, I buried my ankles in the flowerbed After the scattering of countless seeds, unripened buds festered, trapped inside themselves When I opened the trickling roots and rotting taproots to draw out the fluids of sleep, sharp hairs burrowed inward

Were they all hallucinations Fevered bodies that tossed and turned to call for another, that finally passed out from strong liquor into a tangle, that looked at each other with

faces collapsing
shamefully,
eyes falling
as rotten fruit

When humans swallow runny resin in fear of flowers blooming, do their eyes rot without having fruited When I opened my mouth, my tongue grew blotted with double flowers *I'm shy I'm shy* A deformed season when drunken flower stems sway and throw up their guts Inside the flowerbed where I opened my ankle and planted my hot seed

DROPLETS KNOCKING

Knock
Knock

It's a call to someone, the desire for the rim of an ear There used
    to be a time when we called to loved ones with only sound
    When I gently knocked on your forehead, they opened and
    looked up

Your eyes

Inside the two holes
that grew warm and wet around my hands,

there used to be a time when we swam as each other's fluids,
when we loved the perfectly sealed room

I heard a knock with every blink
I gazed at you My eyes lost focus for you to be reborn in double,
    triple vision

When you breathed — *life* — into summer
it began through a crack in the door

PALKKUMCHI

It's the kind of bad weather that only seeps into the corners of
    your body When a flock of birds descend upon a sprawling
    forest, what is this impulse to pull closer whatever you'll send
    farthest away Though the whirling body's gravity remains in
    the embrace

When I call the exterior of a sprained arm, a mind that has
    strayed from the body,

some things bear beautiful labels like the names of typhoons as
    they move toward fatality If I must, I want to fail beautifully
    When I scatter every joint in my body like a vase toppling
    from the table, when I become a windowpane shaking, chest
    open to the storm,

transparent aches drip from my body as I squander the climate,
    waiting for catastrophe When I unravel and unravel a ball of
    thread damp-dark like a drowned plant's feet, I find the core
    of blood that I used to coil to send my mind far far away
    Like a bowstring trembling Like a pitcher's injured shoulder

The moment my protest-sealed lips rip open,
they become a forest crowded out by trees, a core cast away by
    corners, and

grow far away
at the speed they were loved, with just as much force

PERSONAL RAIN

It's true, we touched under each of our own roofs. I can hear the sound of small daggers clanging in my chest. Rain that touches the world's shadows and molds light. Rain that disappears as it burns watery candles all around.

Is the rain a contagious disease? Eyebrows whirling? Sheets of paper that have lost their way? Translucent fingers breaking free from the black ring. Today there are many hands that have dropped their promises.

Under our roofs that overlap and push against each other. If I release a day's worth of rainfall that's been subdivided and stored in every umbrella,

that place is my territory; it is not your time. The fair, fluid fingers trickling from between the sleeve of your stained shirt, your walk home, your tenderness.

We walk beautifully. We're alike, but we're not one. Umbrellas are always slower than rain, just as thoughts are always slower than blood.

To be alike means to be close. I'm pale, and you're pallid. I'm alone, and you're only one. We're similar, but we're not the same. We fit our roofs together and walk a little closer through the lasting rain.

TASTE OF FLOUR

We spared our words for a long time, licking ice
by the window where we cut cake and day drank

Ruining that fragile white outline
you spoke of nonexistent beauty
Carelessly waving your hands
you talked about the letters *f* and *l*

And I, about what crumbles from being clear and distinct like
    grains,
about what becomes uniform particles

Why do they crumble and wander and end up an awful lump

Those snowflakes stained whether I
blew on them or swept them away with my hand
We mourned every white powder
by the window where the refrozen snow was mottled gray

The season of such mourning passes by

I thought all powders would melt away like snow
but it stubbornly stuck to my tongue
So dirty and sad and heavy

ARDENTLY

Hands that hug at the same time question each other's rhythm

There was a fondle that resisted the inner arm The dance of
    fingers sliding down slopes Attenuated shadows glide past
    in a pack

When you boiled down a small tree and applied it to the darkest
    part of your body, the spaces between your bones shrank
    irreversibly Those charred days when we mimicked each
    other's feelings and offered up a different branch

Did someone pluck your tongue and plant a young fish in its
    place Whenever we try to blend our voices, unconfessed
    questions swim out instead

Those were the days when we replaced kisses with the sound of
    fish licking the dry riverbed The days when we became each
    other's impurity and exploited the seasons

SLEEPING WATERS

Rain poured down
shattering faces everywhere

A raindrop's heart, the perfection of a gas

We face each other
with expressions that could
row a boat forward

Black flowers lie beneath the surface
Peering into the tangled waters
I grow shallow

From growing depths
the outline of a flower
unfurls and lifts its leaves
Soft footprints
drag ripped fabric along

When water slips through
summer's channel, lies down,
and abandons its borders

we watch
words as they are
mashed inside a mouth

Melting, the perfection of an emotion

When I held the cup
expressions poured under my feet

Do the best consolations require indifference

The moment red becomes runny, the moment runny becomes a
    query, the time everything thins into a silent syllable

When shadowless leaves soar
the wet coat of the soul
swells and oozes

The perfection of the sleepy surface
brings forth the hidden paths inside the body

UNEXPECTED VANILLA

It glided along the groove of my ear. Vanilla on the tip of my
   tongue, dribbling down the subtle bumps.

We had to keep a neutral expression while scraping all those
   seeds. With a fluttering heart, we memorized the names of
   foreign countries. Our first sensation of sweetness. A special
   appetite for impermanent things.

Yes, some hands and knees were melting. We created each other,
   strokes running hot and cold. In the territory of sound I'm
   a flower reclining vertically. Blossoming before a fingertip.
   The word *embrace* melts and melds upon contact.

That type of vanilla. To keep my eyeballs moist, I love most
   whom I don't know. Some eyelids grew whole the moment
   we lost them. Slid and waved their gentle tentacles before
   falling, heavy with wet.

NO PANTIES

Clinging to trivial promises I lost a leaf

The railing lost my laundry which flapped and stained everywhere
Petals sullied so soon after being washed and hung out to dry

How can I cross this season without a single pair of panties
When I offered a swaying green to every fingertip
and warmed them with my lips
a pair of hands wove underwear from that futile fabric

The lining of spring, the season
that uncovers the body at the slightest breeze

It was a season that didn't require underwear
Days departed and footprints turned transparent
in the kingdom where I started a revolution for one
When I with drunken eyes spoke of both love and refusal
my naked calves trembled with shame

We evaporate soaking our hands in a flower bowl
The flowers that flipped skirts
now throw themselves over the far shoulder of the sun
in the garden where trees take off their panties and wave them
    like flags

FOREPLAY WITH THE HORLA

Hand me a match.
Dear Horla, who named the moment a continuously burning
segment and fell into suspension.

Because I have a fragile name
your gaze is perilous to me.

When you predict the long night to come
leave it, Blanche[1]
She's finally complete today.

Feed her long firm bread
and floating myrrh.

Horla, you bump into me.
Abandoning your lips and face
you turn to look at my back.

The night we fell asleep together
I saw one-legged soldiers outside the window
crowding into the threadleaf cypress forest.
As if they had anything left to lose.

A body that has weathered severe pain
is full of beautiful scrap paper.

---

[1]   Maupassant's physician.

By the time I fumbled to the next seat
the white hemp handkerchief was already gone.
Goodbye, goodbye, from my fingertips.

INSIDE THE TOWER

I rose from sleep and descended an endless flight of stairs.
Abandoning my lamp and wetting my heels in red, I went
round and round the spiral staircase ... but the stairs started
up again and the golden bell I'd stolen grew heavier

If I were gifted too much light, I'd probably soon enter a stain
When I press my ears against these stone walls and call out
to distant birds, trees spread their arms with all their bodies'
despair Why am I inside this absence The sleeper is still at
the top of the whirling tower

When I store the stolen darkness in my eyes and keep rolling
my limbs into my body, it feels like sunlight has reached the
eyebrows I planted far away Like I've stepped inside a new
tower where the stairs only continue upward

If I were to pluck my feathers to write all the things I want to,
I'd probably soon lose my wings and collapse dead on my
scribbles Having become the beast of the bell tower that
gained sound and gave light, I ring the now enormous bell
Until my fingers crumble Until my face becomes sound
Until everything that fell from the bell shakes the tower and
promptly knocks it down

HALF THE BLOOD

Yes I saw the river redden as it parted

When I locked my body with the first key
and opened the blood-gates with the second

flowers poured out through a crack in the night
fading as they met in this strange new kingdom

Flowers erupt through the body
Today I call blood leaking from vessels
the lips of an adulteress

When I stroke my cheek with one hand
and erase my forehead with the other

the evening bleeds out

like lovers parting at the border
like the sun collapsing with its face on the water
blurring the boundaries of the world

A STANDSTILL ORDER

The sailors fetch opium from the shipwreck. Down in the ocean
   trench, we are sunken sinners holding figs in our mouths.
   Budding only inward, weeping only inward.

We shall never reach the shore. Burnt brambles left in the
   charcoal fire. Footprints sink into the black floor. The royal
   guards left in tears. Covering their eyes with the waves' dirty
   linen. Soaking their maps as they waded far. Far beyond this
   place.

A bell tolls from beyond the horizon ... When I think of the
   darkening ramparts, a ray from a distant lighthouse burgeons
   like a bramble. As the guards raise their torches high from
   below the rising waters.

I bite the fruit I held in my mouth for a long time and chew its
   seeds. Borders of water. Obedience of water. Watchtower
   of water. We will never reach that bright coast again. From
   this kingdom where feet grow faint and only lost footprints
   fill the shore.

UNDER THE SHADOW OF YOUR HAND

Sunlight sinks below the created shadow
inside the brief leaf
where your worried forehead and words overlap

Such colors are worrisome
How could they connect the bleak black bloods and store them
    in their palms

My eyes are stained from gazing
at the profile now unfamiliar The stain sticks to my face

When a determined mind makes a cliff
do the gestures make an early grave out of summer

With a face that looks ready to burst with light
I gaze at the lips only half there

Your wreath, my dead flowers

UNRECORDED DAYS

A pale herd of plankton fly across the awakened night The
   whirling flagella, the wanderers, reproach their soft bodies

You've come so far Hanging over the sea fan colony that thickens
   with the trees and tides, the plankton calls to the forgotten
   handwriting

When the fabric woven with wrinkled water and foam sinks
   layer by layer
the moon draws closer As the covert twist of a phantom muscle

There were days when I was transmitted to a blank space and
   learned concealment spells, nights when I enunciated
   shameful words Each time, the surface grew taut and dirty
   and thin Like a sheet of paper the eraser eventually tears
   through

It's as if I had a dream where I was stuttering and bashful Rolling
   my tongue farther and farther inside as it gradually lost color

LOSS OF LIGHT

On the day of the harvest ceremony I wanted to wash the bottom
with melted snow and for my forehead to disappear forever

When I burned my lashes and offered the scent, dry bubbles rose
inside my mouth, which was like experiencing the moon for
the first time I believed that the day I sewed the wall with
a needle tomorrow's promise would be tied to the hand of
the dead

There were four eyes looking at each other with black fabric
between them
Inside a throat growing infinitely deeper

When I bury my face in the fading gaze, white birds flee to a
thickening forest and my lover's collar stains brightly Look
at the gaze of the blind applause following me all the way
into my dreams

I undo all my braids and let them get wet Until the eerie river
flows and a ringing in someone's ears echoes from elsewhere
Until the frost fallen on my heart drips thick and dark

TRACE

The time of field heaping when ashes dance
Footprints cannot have roofs
so long wanderings always head to a cliff

I touch the rust pattern on the barberry tree as I walk
Through the crack in my forehead my red insides
can be seen and I grow lighter by the handful
like a lean sack filled with dust

Pushing through thickets I reach the land
where strangers met before
left behind warmth indiscreetly

Where did we all hide our bodies,
having become detailed insensible inklings

I multiply as I am erased
I fear all my eyelashes will disappear

I didn't notice that I started hiding my hands
like the pharmacist wrapping powder medicine in paper
so I won't shatter and be swept away

TASTE OF WINGS

This is the story of two equal tongue-tips,
of white double flowers laid on lips.

Rain yesterday, snow today. Ashen snowflakes rush into fading
sleep. Unaware of your darkness, you proceed. To an embrace
not mine. Ice melting, the slow loosening of folded wings.
Shoulders spread as though they'd been waiting. Shoulders
bloom. I feel like my hands will disappear. Because of the
person who says they can have you. Because of the colors
that dye the corners of my eyes then dim.

I watch these crystal decisions dissolve to the very end. I feel
like every eyelash will scatter. I'd wanted to shed my shadow
by flying high and far. Unaware of the snowflake, I wait for
the snowflake. The taste of wings that dissolve on the tip of
my tongue. All that melts after freezing is lonesome. In this
world where rain turns to snow then rain again, ruining all
that is white.

I hear the sound of white bells clanging against each other inside
the soaring liquid. Where did you abandon the snowflake
on which I wrote my secrets? It rained yesterday and it's
snowing today. What's sadder: the world that freezes or the
world that melts away?

JUST AS THE MAGNOLIA
DOESN'T KNOW ITS OWN LIMIT

I smell rotten flowers when I hug you Black gums line up as long
as we kiss Oh dear horrible odors collected on my worn-
out bed The partially dead air falls, stained, across from the
people

The white season arrives, stepping on dead genitals When I
provide a dwelling between moments and offer a disappearing
room, the season forecasts a full bloom only after scrapping
its fingers and grasping at the empty spaces Your lips part,
strewing this night with what are newborn and white

Abandoned flower petals squirm as pallid tongues and come to
forget their own color Just as trees don't know the green
they have Just as the snowflake resting on a newly born
corpse doesn't know its own temperature

Crescent moons softening and browning wherever fingernails
dug in The gaze gone bad, expelling white discharge
Partially dead moon halos They all pour into and lurk inside
that deep dark maw

UNDER THE FLUTTERING
RED AND WHITE FLAGS[2]

After I gave birth to a boneless child and lit living greens on fire,
    the white laundry grew bloodied Carmine, crimson, the
    smell of a neighbor's burning skin from over the mountain

When I stepped into the room with charcoal-blackened feet,
    the shroud I was weaving suddenly faded away, its threads
    coming loose Are you crossing to the far side with a long
    long thread wrapped around your wrist, dear newborn, dear
    newdead

Limp fruits hang from every branch of the locust tree fighting to
    toss their leaves Those slack spineless things, hit by a stone
    and releasing the crimson wave

It was a cold, bleak neighborhood The night I slept with the
    dull knife that cut the umbilical cord, red pus flowed from
    the lunar halo all night Like a conception dream that goes
    on and on

---

2 홍백기: Flags flown outside the home of every Korean shaman,
marking the connection between the spiritually gifted *mudang* and
the heavens.

SUMMER, WHEN I DREAMT OF VINES

I pick up a fallen trumpet flower and rub it on my eyes
and now I'm inside the light as I wished

When I dream of summer and feel around the water
light's interior opens wide

Sleep is like an old castle
covered in vines, its silhouette forgotten

A flower created from flipping and stitching up summer
When the flower offers scarlet and turns itself inside out
the water's moment
dips its waist underground and dreams of a different position

A flower, a dream dreamt by water borrowing color
Spouting strange bumps
above the black stone wall surrounded by old blossoms,
the vines of summer extend countless tendrils

When I climb the wall of sultry sleep
like eyeless leaves

the fingers of light
pour onto my eyes

I roll my lips inward and hold my breath
and now I'm inside the dream, the water-dream as I wished

Hong of deep waters, they said. The tender loneliness of the person with water in their surname draws near. Releasing papers, scattering a tree's concentration. The surface sinks. I watch the wandering branches. Wrinkled waters flow under my tongue. It's wide enough for names to be slowly undone.

The touch of my hand dyes the water's surface, I wrote. The waterside of summer when I created unbelievable stories according to the pattern on a stained shirt. Breaths growing heavy inside your body when you offered a handful of water, circles wanting to grow alike. Rolling closer like an hourglass, as slowly as the body leans. *What if I misbehaved? What if I ran away?* you ask, and look at me.

Water grows up to be a dewdrop at the tip of a thought. Can you believe that whispers consult humidity and the atmosphere in order to flow? That trees created bark patterns and heart ripples to hand us secrets? When you squash the secrets that curve like question marks and hand them over, curious waters are born where tongue and uvula meet. The waters are extremely deep.

About the kindnesses dirtying the earth's surface. About the kisses recovered by the sleep's surface. When a note you'd sent long ago resurfaces on the waterside today, there's a name that keeps expanding. Can you believe that? I whisper in the rippling ear, *I'm heading out to a water level unknown to the person who planted a tree inside their surname.*

UNDERWATER JUNGLE

I watch the grapes swell
slowly taking in the water
I feel like a juicy fruit
overripe in the flower basin

A forest
composed of
bubbles speaking

There, we are fish flicking scales
fish climbing trees
When we lead sticky swaying shadows

and rub our fins:
the bumps soar
the tongue pounds

Inside the water's perfect embrace
I hide my face about to scatter
like the plant with a developed back

Sprouting at my fingertip, the hand again

STAR, SICK

Why do certain nights smudge like charcoal while other times
shatter and become glittering glass shards When I open my
mouth filled with ice and call out your paled name,

I accidentally chew on some alien rocks Must I compile ominous
tattoos by carving the black powder of night into my body
and build a shrine for bygone dreams When I hid stars
shattered under my tongue, all the rocks inside my body
shone moonward

When I burn a stranger's fingernails and inhale the smoke, I
feel as though I've gained a different body Look, lights are
seeping into my bones and melting down deep Why do
sparks fly when certain bodies collide, why do certain bodies
remain stains inside dreams

UNTOUCHABLE

I put my hands inside another's pulp and stirred deep. My arms dyed black. The contaminated light shone bright, exposing my hand's mistake.

Some had been entrusted. Those thrown out while clutching unfamiliar branches. Who cut their flawed hair and buried it in the heap of thicket and grass.

Having become their narrow sticky dwelling, I walk with sound before me. When I grow countless toes and gain a mushed gait, every morning has become abundant with mouthless teeth. There was the poison of flesh rubbing impiously. A person walking as they etched a beautiful delicate pattern on their bare back.

When I covered my body with a pile of white grass, the powders surged and covered the teary surface of an eye. When you, with your most tender exterior, fester at the slightest embrace and easily trickle, there was a place we had to find while washing our footprints.

Disappear, carrying high a jar holding a thin bodily fluid. Looking like some dirty petal blooming and wilting. Revolve and return, having become a strange stitch contaminating the shadow. Stir the well of night and swim with every knuckle swirled in that mire.

FLOWERANTLER

When it pressed the white floor
it became a low tree
it became a sudden icicle

Was its sleep unsound A shallow footprint brushing between
    the brows

When I created a seam as if it were new textile
the memory of the root would protrude out of shock

The leftover flesh is pitiful The confession that melted
then hardened when the wind returned puts down its mild blade

Isn't it rare When I open the door of mucilage
that trembled at every caress and lay my body down,

I weave and weave: the dream of earning identical whirls
and rubbing the newly sprouted sexes
atop last year's linen

A MOMENT'S HAND

Every second of waiting became a knife

Watching time be born and born again,
Aah, I created a voice
I fiddled with for a long time in my hand

Dearly clutching dozens of blades,
feeling like I'm sprouting another finger

DAYS OF HUMIDITY

On nights I planted fog in every fingertip, I'd open the window
like I was touching the foot of a drowned person

Those days, I'd fall asleep under an overcoat patched with wet
cotton

The dwelling of murky blood can only be reached by scattering
all the moisture inside the body into the air The person who
swam inside me drifted to a moment's sea A bizarre world
where you must be soaked to touch the end of a sentence

When fog gathers around my stiffened tongue, my mouth grows
foggy as if stuffed with cornflowers Inside the feather of a
bird brushing its shoulders off, the seasons suddenly became
an old superstition

BEHIND THE DOWNPOUR

The other side stopped tossing and turning for a moment. Taking off their flower crown, the young god looks down at the long loose coat they've dragged along. The night is intermittent.

The blindness of vegetation casts a low curtain inside the body. Flowers scattered like broken glass shards await the god's bare feet.

All that feels possible is here.[3] Above the distant branch is the one who went home after knocking on the window all day. Just when the planets born out of friction turn their backs on each other.

Things were about to be decided over there. Fading shadows fell wherever tree intestines had been swept away. Leaves made of water. Today, we must suffer this damp divulging of the universe.

---

3   from George Bacovia's "Noise".

NIGHT, LIKE A PRINT

There's a kingdom we must reach before the magnolias wilt
    We dragged our wet feet along the stone path that led to
    the riverside Following the spread of countless fine cracks,
    everything flowed in the opposite direction of day

Did my letter about infinite ridges awaken you to your limitations?
    Did someone scatter bone dust gathered overnight across
    the sky? Is that why the settled ashes are swirling into a
    frightening complex pattern?

When I overlay sheets of stone and achieve a clear chiaroscuro,
    I caress the excavated feet and look at the landscape realized
    through intaglio The pale faces of magnolias hanging from a
    black branch, the patterns engraved with a sharpened bone,
    the roof of the night I pulled something old into my arms
    — From this bright place rife with white and black powders

I turn my gaze
to a world of ever-embroidered stains

By any chance, is the bygone light only now shining on your
    naked back? When we wore our shadows like shrouds and
    touched the magnolias dyed black, bright chisels emerged at
    the tips of our sharp fingernails It shone above the roof of
    the night we tried fitting our shadows together

PULVIS[4]

We tell ourselves apart by patterns of sickness

Spare feelings
    Spare songs

    Little
by little

becoming clearer

shaken

       shaken

fingers pour out

Since I've spread you out in the sun today,

goodbye

       goodbye,

dear countless bodies turning to dust

---

4   *pulvis*: meaning both "dust" and "stage" in Latin.

SENSE OF SNOWFLAKES

Warm was the winter I spent with the plumber.

By night, snowflakes were born over the wall
as I tossed frozen branches into the fireplace
and heard the trees stretching their chilly toes.

The limbs of souls dyed cold
when I scattered scrap metal out the window.

Winter's plumbing
faded
like antique jewelry, most beautiful when thrown away.

You put your ear to my wrist
and called over the water pipes buried in a distant land.

I forgot my features like a stiffening droplet
and thought of veins, as my hands and feet were slowly snapped
    off.

To keep from freezing
I needed a steady flow of tears.

Ashen trees were molded wherever the snowstorm reached.
Forcing broken fingers into the fireplace,
we hugged the wet trees and went up in flames.

I SAW YOUR WIFE

When a failed romance reaches winter, I hurl the dirtied words
far and splatter the fence *I saw your wife* I am a stain, having
become a little or lifeless child

From the perspective of you who are falling, do familiar
sensations darken your blood and bones? As you soak your
body in various lips and wield the night, certain questions
freeze up after secretly melting Then a blizzard is the inside
of flower clusters pushing and pestering each other Drifting
and swelling and drifting and soaring

Dates falling from a calendar into a puddle get trapped in the
stained clump of snow and mutter to themselves Like a pet
rejected by his Master or a snowman that doesn't melt

Some things are degraded by lingering When I try to wipe the
expression off my face, my eyes and nose mudslide Fearful
words now fill my mouth Can I call it a stolen room, or a
cliff

ODALISQUE ON THURSDAY

My dear mistress[5], the silk-polished jewels are refracted into a
thousand layers. Oh odalisque, you apply rose-apple juice to
your lips and forget how to speak.

Is it the holy day of almonds crunching as you clench your
teeth? Despite having been estranged early in life and lost
many cycles, the night becomes the domesticated animal of
soft gums because there is a certain warp thread even on
discontinuous days.

When you stomp on the water's decision with your bare heel,
the pattern becomes an emotion that seeps through. On the
day the empty space and the spoiled place overlap, the day
the foreign substance inside a jewel is called the climate, the
newly urgent Thursday suddenly gathers into a single point.

Mistress eyes the curve of the wet red ear. The orderliness of
a friendly low rib. The relationship between bed and skin,
akin to needle and fuzz. On the day of the week that reaches
the sadness of the nape.

---

5   A female slave who serves the sultan. Every Friday the sultan must
attend the queen's bedchamber.

STAR OF PERFIDY[6]

Waving dirty handkerchiefs the flowers set off, and a rotten
summer is hung above the gibbet. Oh cruel green, fronds
throwing spring as far as possible. Through a crack in the
unfortunate world the sticky night is sprouting once again,
I see.

My praying bitch, I am wearing a wilted laurel wreath and
watching the stars crash down. Casting a wet forest under
my tear ducts. Darkness finally earns its share when it forgets
its starry discernment and the past by taking sickness as its
true nature.

The time when beards grow ferociously, the first quarter
moon outside the metal fence looks like my cute bone.
Like a miniaturist who draws absence with a finger sliding
downhill, a delicately pointed brush tip, I always arrive at
the fearful place.

Sensing, sobbing, we're inside such darkness but I have suns that
rise in herds. Stars that soon change and grow abundant in
my hand … If lips are graves made daily, bones must be our
final burial clothes. But there is no night for those who close
their eyes.

Newly sprouted stars are deserting this night, I see. A burning
veil will soon cover your forehead and make it rot. Even if

---

6   From Sade's *Juliette* (tr. Austryn Wainhouse). "Star of perfidy, your
ascendant places all else in eclipse, smothers all else in me save the
longing for crime and infamy…"

your voice expires your respiration will remain and return as
God's inhalation. Like a curtain of an afternoon that billows
then settles anon.

EVENING, WHEN MY PET
PLANT OPENS ITS EYES

Your breaths tangled when a leaf sprouted from every orifice

When you dangled these abnormal leaves and waited for a full
moon

the liquids flowing through the xylem swelled in unison

as pupils multiplied and countless lips parted

When you become the evening's mung bean sprout and release
ominous shadows

do roots flow out from where your hands and feet were twisted

There's a saying that a creature born in the night must bear much
darkness

Since they bloom facing the west and take their final breath
looking at the ground

may the poisonous be as beautiful as they wish

On this night you quietly bled white blood, waiting for the day
of destruction

FLOWER BASIN

Was the light spilled by the summer fruit It was bright all night
 inside the bones,

now something hot and sticky is suddenly leaking past my lips

Was it because I kissed the wet roots again and again and

stole half of them in my mouth

All day my mouth reeked of freshly cut grass and rotting flowers

full of green moss tangled under my tongue

so perhaps we are truly old plants

Only after holding back its layers of bodily fluids faded from
 countless dilution

and getting wet down to its roots, the moon earns fists of rust

The bodily fluids, or waves, bloomed by the moon reach a
 boundary

and detailed patterns seep from its wet body

Meanwhile between toes that multiply

and water vines that grow even when spat out

lips barely float down

looking as if they've earned some small peculiar berry

A BOIL ON MY HAND

It smelled of ripped grass

You sweep your fingertips
almost as if to pull up a past life

I cross over toward some other flesh
like the lost final piece
of a beautifully complex puzzle

Wild grass sprouted with their ears cut off
wherever I clipped my nails

Breaths
become brilliant
by braving bucking temperatures

How does pain come to claim authority?

Smelling the scent secreted
from cutting each other out,

you called yourself dirty
I think the truly dirty write
some version of this on their blank pages

I tried my best to be beautiful

The wind inside my hand kills what's raw

New gods are born in every pained direction

Are we human? If we are,
will this ever be possible?

you asked, touching the hand turned unfamiliar

RECEIVING THE RUNNY RED GEM

You said you found a snowflake that never melts
the home of the blister growing day by day

We held our breath to erase the boundary of air
Then strange blood seeped
from our tangled tongues and laced fingers

I lowered my head and hid my tongue
until sticky juices dripped between our lips

When I molded the oozing
sap into a secret seed

a berry began to swell
the small warm berry that never wore down
however many times I rolled it around in my mouth

THE NIGHT BEHIND THE WINDOW

The waters shattered when I closed my eyes. When I close the window and look at the flowing outdoors, the curtain of the wind is endlessly unfurled from the ill mind. The interior of the world forms a lump of unknown color.

The wet nights lounge along the length of my eyes. Do we transcribe the blotches with our blinking eyelids because the body also holds a needed darkness? When I lower the curtain immeasurable words are blurred behind the window.

Dear you turning off the lights and pulling the covers to dive inside yourself every night. Dear you all laboring a fixed amount of darkness. A night when what shatters to shine is scattered. When you press your hands against your closed eyes the kaleidoscope of night turns slowly.

Where did the flapping windows of summer go. Darkness sinks into the rotating body, and I close my eyes and gather my embrace toward the pitch dark. Between breath and breath, in the direction the heart dyes.

AMOK

We're still alive. If eyes are the muzzle of a gun, then they're also dark moons shut from inside. When we open our eyes, bullets of light pour out from the two holes getting hideously deeper.

Can we call them molten bones?

Amok, we rush ahead. Feeling like the crowns of our heads are lighting up. So we can get warm even without sincerity. So we can receive glances that dart even without their eyeballs. So we can dump our blood and enter deep inside the heart. Having become the missing child and injured fools collapsing at the front door of a dream.

In that moment, we're beautiful like water droplets gliding across an oily puddle. Can we call them a moment's jewels? Amok, catch the moment when blazing branches shine limpid. Trees swarming. Gunshots embracing a chest by the force of insanity.

I'm dying. Amok, even as I blink and pull the trigger, the bullet is only fired inward. When you tug at my heartstrings from the outside, watch the hairs of my mad trees flutter in flames.

SPRINKLER

When you look closely at a bruise, a beam of darkness seems to
    shine from inside your body. All the spots you've bumped
    darken belatedly like shots fired at a runaway prisoner, and

the garden deepens.

A tree stands in a corner of the garden. Wearing pointy heels,
    sinking its feet into the mud.

If a plant could remove its shoes of soil, it'd probably first escape
    this violence of water. Away from the deep shadowy gloom
    pooling inside the rain-making umbrella.

The body with many footnotes is sad.
Like how all your old bruises will resurface when you die.

The water stream swirls violently. My knees are soaked in soil.
    Branches draped with shiny leaves.

The leaves of grass whisper among themselves, wearing a kitten
    heel on each root. The tree, dyed black, sinks down. Deep
    into the soil until it reaches just below its chin. The tree
    throws off its earrings and necklaces and bracelets. Once the
    heels come off, bare feet fade out to blue.

The tree sank here. Can I call this the root of the bruise? And
    the sprinkler continues to turn, until the garden becomes
    one bruised blue.

LALALA, CHERRIES

Hello, I'm going cherry picking I want to fill my pockets with
only the ones stained dark Cherries are red copying another
red Shall we fill our mouths with cherries and kiss naughtily
knottily all night long

Cherries strip off their flowers and leaves Today they're just
kernels of play

Her cherry hasn't even had a chance to ripen and burst, to
schmooze and ooze We only got to bite into a clump of
green And now the season's almost over We were harvested
too soon I want to swirl my paints inside her mouth This is
the time of cherries A time that stains

UNDER TWO LAYERS OF CURRENTS

I fell asleep using a leaf as my pillow Inside the water-forest
    where netted dreams sway and part tens of thousands of lips

Feeling like I have a swim bladder that melts away, I watch the
    shadow flip over When I stick my tongue far out and feel out
    the dark water's interior, the rim of an ear grows abundant
    and the bubbling bubbles bloom towards the surface

When I set down my breath and beckon the dream of gravity,
    the gap disappears from inside sleep A herd of bubbles was
    born below tilted lashlines The depths of April grow deep
    even before getting wet

I'll prepare the blood and flowers and bring over the powers of
    a distant place Today as a massive vortex is born inside the
    open mouth of someone buried at sea

FISH TANK HOLDING A SEA ROBIN

Did you see my hesitant lips The single knot tied with dozens
    of strands

of luster so that clear scales would form under my skin

Where are the footless born? There was

a translucent membrane spread between each swelling finger

Giving a sidelong glance at the blackened water,

that red chest burning up at last, I spoke of the bottom's business

Should I sing, with my pants' drawstrings loosened and my
    bedding hanging out?

Inside the fish tank where someone else's sap was released

who was entirely yours? Your posture as your

curved spine moving through the invaded water

and the dim scales that poured out and flooded in

Rotting is a passion, too: promising nothing,

you escape towards the water's far shoulder

Yours is a body that blazes again each day

CROSSING THE BLACK PAGE OF SLEEP

Dear child, who fell asleep crying:
They rip sleep along the slant of your eyes.

You grew up crouching like the dog ear
of a page that grew ominously wet.

Dear child, who fell asleep cursing someone:
Dreams embroider the repeated stains
of night between your furrowed brows.

Riding the long twine down the slant of your eyes,
you enter the stacked sheets of dreamscape.
Hands rifling through the curtains of a thick night.
Black lumps seep into my mouth and ears.

The moment darkness was cut out
and my whole body was lifted into the air.
The moment the sharp light and breath dug into your body.

Dear child, who lost a shoe in slumber
and now flees in tears:
Limping, you recall
the warm ankle
that must still be inside your shoe.

Should I call that the soul,
or the body of a dream?

Dear child, who died in a dream:
The droplets of sorrow lead you to two doors.
One closes repeatedly.
The other constantly ripped out.

FEMDOM

Fish grew in every corner of the room and cultivated a sharp light. Bodies riddled with needle marks. Those that fled and returned are sticking their heads out again and thirsting for scars. Those laboring genitals. Bodies fainting inside my net. Look at the wet scales swimming towards the ripples of expulsion. Look at the broken fingers knocking on the door bolted shut. When I tenderly trample on the trembling gaze of another being to become their master, all my luminous fish cry out with tied feet. That's the gift of fear. My beautiful low-lives, who pledge allegiance only after opening their veins and checking for a surge. Look at these epitaphs flopping all over the bedroom floor. All day long I rip and break the half-dead yesterdays. With fear led by an even larger fear.

SPROUTING BONES

When I dug through the dirt-covered ceiling with my itchy
    fingertips, a cold light leaked in through the new hole

The ankle buried in a grave resurfaced on melted snow When I
    stroke its blackened toes, runny bits of flesh and the peculiar
    smell of frozen things melting are secreted

The opaque spring that dripped profusely between ribs
Those lips that vanished without a trace after starting so many
    rumors Because only the dead may grow out their nails[7],
    even the tip of a rotten genital is budding to extend its first
    leaf

The freshest body stands on the rotten flesh
Hold the faint hand, so the newly acquainted bones can soar

---

7   From Herta Müller's *Nadirs* (tr. Sieglinde Lug).

USE OF GREEN

How beautiful plants are Stirred and
releasing color inside hot water

the leaf's held breath
deepens for a moment then unfurls

Whoever freed a plant in boiling water
was the first drink that color

Who linked a tree crown to their veins
in attempt to understand blood?

I think about them drinking
the cooled plant to make green wander
and the satellites of blood

inside the boiling air

ERASABLE SEEDS

Tonight I've curled up with a grape in my mouth. With black liquids overflowing from a dream, the grape sheds its tender skin and sinks deep into the earth. Even as the seeds I swallowed without chewing have suffused my bones, transplanting my blood vessels with tiny roots. A plant's quilt, weaving roots long and thin. When I understand trees and cradle my bones, my skin disappears and my body melts in many directions. I love ripe things. The things that get helplessly squished in between. But could I love your bones? White tree bark protruding from a scraped knee. A seed is not the afterlife of a tree, but the original piece that's been lost. When a grape seed gradually flows into the root, it fits the last puzzle piece, completing the tree. I know there are faces spreading ceaselessly, just as green seeps out of a dead fence. I know there is a newly thickening forest. Extending our grapevines, we kiss. To find the small, hard seed inside each other's bodies. We melt it in our mouths for a long, long time before swallowing.

THE NEIGHBORHOOD

See you soon
It smelled of the slightly dark park

The heart wanders then fades
The park's footprints
are too close to reach

Kind neighbors are inside Sunday
and dwindling greetings
carry split body temperatures but

what did we have What made us melt
Those words split open from the left

See you soon See you soon

at the park where trees assemble colorful gestures
to complete an unfamiliar word

Lips melt with the thought of promises
like a late spring squandering its life's worth of lilac

ALBINO

When you dive into a bubble
your fingerprints melt underwater

There was a bleached breath
Like a heart beating inside a mouth

When the spare afternoon flowed to the dark
I hugged the lily-white shadow
the glass body

Inside the body filling with light
the delicate wings of fish

You have updates growing gradually transparent
Go shine as if you swim only once before you sleep

Until the emaciated moon
like a long fingernail
grows into the body

SOMEONE FROM THE WESTERN RIVERSIDE

They left letting red water into their tail Some things can walk
only at night The sunset returns to every sparse blight and
lies down long The anchorage of such breaths The riverside
where hideous exactingly molded things flow down in a row

When I made a pillow by gathering grains of sand and covered
it in a thin textile I wove by braiding waterweeds, I dreamed
the dream of an insect with vivid nerves in its wings Branches
that only grow inward, footprints of the west that finally
disappear following their desperation

If I dig a hole in every place where bodily fluids have been
sprayed and bury a dim finger, is that the business of the
beyond? They grabbed wandering spores in each hand and
set off trailing layers of clothes Why did they return? There
were round, plenty warm things here

The dead fetus does not know its own flesh There was a person
comprised of traces, like fabric briefly woven then unraveled
Fluid skin leaking, abandoning the breaths sloshing in and
out That deep scar called water

WATER FOOTPRINT

Like leaves that turn wherever a tree has walked past

If I bury my feet underwater and recall the names that grew mild
the tongue unfurls wide

When I held a wilting hand
strange branches grew thick

In the way that water makes plants rise to other heights
like the particles of the blank space that swell up to the wet
    fingertip
there were quiet strides headed outside the body

The heart
that becomes a dimension
when you pierce a hole in a blank sheet of paper and call over
    light

When cloudy things slip out of ice
how far can you go, barely containing the body about to burst

Where does the water droplet released by a wilting plant
rest for the last time

When numerous clock hands roam inside the body
breath is an instrument being born
an instrument that'll soon disappear

Like the ink's sleepy surface just before it evaporates above the
    paper
there were soft bodies
wearing flowing fabric and surging far away, yes

There were clear footsteps growing distant the longer I watched
with a gesture that was neither greeting nor farewell

수면 Sumyeon means both 'sleep' and 'water surface' in Korean. The water's surface represents the state of not knowing, where anything is yet possible.

'There's more room for imagination,' Lee Hyemi told me in a 2019 interview for *Words Without Borders*, the first time we met in person. 'Maybe I like not knowing more than having found out. We say we sink into sleep. We sink into water. We sink into thought. I think all this sinking is related to falling, whether we fall into or for something. The water surface contains the wait of the world before we fall in. To sink into something, you have to start at the surface.'

And at the surface, lips part. In expectation. With questions. The poem 'Cenote' asks, 'Can I call it a hole that reflects darkness? Or a well that draws up the moon?' Another called 'Sprinkler' asks, 'Can I call this the root of the bruise?' These questions of naming have stayed with me because the poems ask for permission where others would have decided and defined. The wait is not a weight here, as the two are homophones only in English.

Meanwhile, I hesitated to cast ripples across the sleepy surface. What if my presence would be nothing but a disturbance? What prevailed over my nerves was my desire to submerge myself in the radical illogic of *Unexpected Vanilla* that defies physical reality and social mores ever so nonchalantly. To translate, I had to see what she imagined: not only the elsewheres but the elsehows. The way an umbrella can be a roof, the way seeds can be invitations into dreams. I thank Lee Hyemi for her friendship over the years, as there is much I wouldn't have known had she not answered my questions of renaming and guided me through her world of the second person.

Charlotte Mandell, who translates from French to English, has written about translating surrealist poetry and the significance of priming, or 'the process by which the order in which images appear triggers perception in the brain.' Translating from Korean to English poses additional challenges in regard to syntax, especially in lineated poems where the exact order of images is impossible to relay into grammatical English due to the different word order. This weighed on me, until I learned to sink with that weight. Fragments became complete sentences, and vice versa. Parts of speech transmuted. Register, in the absence of honorific conjugations, was adjusted with phrases like 'It's true' or 'Hello.'

Like I wrote in the first edition, 'I like what the water shows me / when I'm deep inside.' Who isn't seduced by the surface and its possibilities? But diving into this book gifted me so many precious experiences, including in-person readings before it even became a book in English and virtual events with readers quarantining yet communing all around the world. It made me a published translator! Descension carries a negative valence in a world that lives by the conceptual metaphor that up is good and down is bad—but writing this note, I'm reminding myself that all ocean exploration (and conservation!) begins with a descent. And one dive makes no expert. There will always be more awaiting us.

Let these poems bewilder you, arouse you into another kind of knowing.

Wink wink,
Soje
August 2022

This edition first published in the United Kingdom by Tilted Axis Press in 2020. This translation was funded by Arts Council England.

Translation and publication supported by a grant from LTI Korea.

tiltedaxispress.com

ISBN (paperback)   9781911284505
ISBN (ebook)   9781911284499

A catalogue record for this book is available from the British Library.

Editor: Deborah Smith
Managing Editor: Theodora Danek
Copyeditor: Saba Ahmed
Publicity: Hana Sandhu, Sana Goyal (2020)
Community Manager: Tice Cin
Foreign Rights Director: Julia Sanches
Publisher: Kristen Vida Alfaro, Deborah Smith (2020)
Cover design, author and translator illustrations: Soraya Gilanni Viljoen
Photograph: Okto Lee
Typesetting and ebook production: Simon Collinson, Abbas Jaffary

Printed and bound by Clays Ltd, Elcograf S.p.A.
Second Printing 2022

Supported using public funding by
ARTS COUNCIL
ENGLAND

ABOUT TILTED AXIS PRESS

Founded in 2015 and based in London and elsewhere, Tilted Axis is a not-for-profit press on a mission to shake up contemporary international literature.

Tilted Axis publishes the books that might not otherwise make it into English, for the very reasons that make them exciting to us – artistic originality, radical vision, the sense that here is something new.

Tilting the axis of world literature from the centre to the margins allows us to challenge that very division. These margins are spaces of compelling innovation, where multiple traditions spark new forms and translation plays a crucial role.

As part of carving out a new direction in the publishing industry, Tilted Axis is also dedicated to improving access. We're proud to pay our translators the proper rate, and to operate without unpaid interns.

We hope you find this fantastic book as thrilling and beguiling as we do, and if you do, we'd love to know.

tiltedaxispress.com

@TiltedAxisPress